Robins

Heather C. Hudak

WEIGL PUBLISHERS INC.
"Creating Inspired Learning"
www.weigl.com

Published by Weigl Publishers Inc.
350 5th Avenue, 59th Floor
New York, NY 10118
Website: www.weigl.com

Library of Congress Cataloging-in-Publication Data available upon request.
Fax 1-866-44-WEIGL for the attention of the Publishing Records department.

ISBN 978-1-60596-922-0 (hard cover)
ISBN 978-1-60596-923-7 (soft cover)

Printed in the United States of America in North Mankato, Minnesota
1 2 3 4 5 6 7 8 9 0   14 13 12 11 10

042010
WEP264000

Editor: Heather C. Hudak
Design: Terry Paulhus

All of the Internet URLs given in the book were valid at the time of publication. However, due to the dynamic nature of the Internet, some addresses may have changed, or sites may have ceased to exist since publication. While the author and publisher regret any inconvenience this may cause readers, no responsibility for any such changes can be accepted by either the author or the publisher.

Every reasonable effort has been made to trace ownership and to obtain permission to reprint copyright material. The publishers would be pleased to have any errors or omissions brought to their attention so that they may be corrected in subsequent printings.

Weigl acknowledges Getty Images as its primary image supplier for this title.

CONTENTS

4   What is a Robin?
7   Nest News
8   Laying Eggs
10   Keeping Warm

13   Breaking Free
14   One at a Time
16   Growing Up
18   Call and Answer
20   Spring Thaw
22   Robin Mobile
23   Find Out More
24   Glossary/Index

What is a Robin?

Have you ever seen a dark bird with a bright red chest sitting on a fence? This may have been a robin. Robins live across North America. They can be found in many **habitats**, such as gardens, forests, and parks.

Like all living things, robins have a life cycle. They hatch, grow to adults, and have babies of their own.

The robin is the state bird of Wisconsin, Michigan, and Connecticut.

Nest News

What type of house do you live in? Robins live in nests. They build nests in trees or bushes that are 5 to 68 feet (1.5 to 20.7 meters) off the ground. The cup-shaped nests are made from twigs, dead grass, and mud. They are large enough to hold a baseball inside.

Females build a nest when they are ready to lay eggs. Males help protect the nest from **predators**. Sometimes, robins dive at people who come near the nest.

Laying Eggs

Have you ever twisted the cap off a pop bottle? A robin's egg is about the same size as a bottle cap. Robins lay one egg a day for three to five days. They do this two or three times a year.

Most birds lay their eggs at sunrise. Robins lay their eggs mid-morning. They spend the early morning hours finding worms to eat. Worms are harder to find once the weather warms up later in the day.

A robin's tiny eggs are usually blue in color. This makes them harder for **color-blind** predators to find.

9

Keeping Warm

Do you ever sit on your hands when they are cold? Robins sit on their eggs to keep them warm. This helps the birds inside grow.

Robins only sit on their eggs once the entire **clutch** has been laid. If they began warming each egg as it was laid, some babies might start growing before others. The eggs hatch after 12 to 14 days.

A mother robin will leave the clutch for only 5 or 10 minutes at a time so that she can search for food.

Breaking Free

Have you ever cracked open an egg? People use their hands to break the shell. Baby robins have a hard "hook" on their beak. This hook is called an egg tooth. Robins use it to break free from the egg.

The baby uses the egg tooth to make a hole in the eggshell. It is hard work to break free. The baby must rest from time to time. It can take a baby robin an entire day to fight its way out of the egg.

One at a Time

How much did you weigh at birth? Most human babies are 6 to 9 pounds (2.7 to 4 kilograms). Baby robins weigh a little less than a 25-cent coin.

In most cases, one baby robin hatches each day. This happens in the same order the eggs were laid. The tiny birds are born blind. They are wet and have no feathers. Baby robins rely on their parents to bring them the food they need to grow strong.

Baby robins stay in the nest for 9 to 16 days after they hatch.

Growing Up

Can human babies jump two weeks after birth? Robins start to jump from the nest at about 13 days of age. It takes 10 to 15 days more for them to become good at flying. Then, they can live on their own.

Full-grown robins have dark outer feathers and a red chest. These birds grow to be 9 to 11 inches (23 to 28 centimeters) long. Their wings stretch more than 1 foot (0.3 m) across.

In nature, robins can live to be six years old.

Call and Answer

How do you know when friends are talking to you? They use your name or speak to you. Robins use special sounds like "cuck" or "tuk" to talk to each other. A "yeep" or "peek" sound warns of danger. A "chirr" sound that slowly gets louder sounds like a laugh.

Robins are known for their singing. Their song sounds like "cheerily cheer-up cheerio." They whistle to make this sound.

Spring Thaw

How do you know it is spring? Do you see melting snow or flowers in bloom? Some people think of robins as one of the first signs of spring.

During winter, the ground freezes. It is hard for robins to find food. Some robins spend the winter **roosting** in trees. Others fly south to places where they can find plenty of food. They return to their summer homes in early spring. This is when the ground has **thawed**. The robins can now find worms to eat.

21

Robin Mobile

crayons   glue   tape   scissors   string

feathers   glitter   empty cereal box   white, green, and blue paper

1. Draw four robins on the white paper. Cut out the drawings, and decorate both sides.

2. Draw a nest on the white paper, and cut it out. Decorate both sides of the nest.

3. Draw six eggs on the blue paper. Cut them out, and glue three on each side of the nest.

4. Draw a treetop on the green paper, and cut it out.

5. Trace the treetop on another piece of green paper, and cut it out.

6. Glue the treetop pictures to cardboard from the cereal box, and cut the box to fit.

7. Cut a slit from the top center of one treetop and the bottom center of the other. Then, slide the pieces together.

8. Cut five pieces of string, and tape one end to each of the bird and nest drawings. Tape the other end to the treetops.

Now, you have a robin mobile.

Find Out More

To learn more about robins, visit these websites.

Journey North American Robin
www.learner.org/jnorth/tm/robin/Dictionary.html

American Robin Facts
http://depts.washington.edu/
natmap/facts/american_robin
_712.html

American Robin
www.kidzone.ws/animals/
birds/american-robin.htm

All About Birds
www.allaboutbirds.org/guide/
american_robin/id

Glossary

clutch: all of a robin's eggs

color-blind: unable to see certain colors or any color at all

habitats: areas where animals live

predators: animals that hunt other animals for food

roosting: settling in a certain place

thawed: melted

Index

beak 13

eggs 7, 8, 10, 13, 14, 22

grow 4, 10, 14, 16

nest 7, 14, 16, 22

singing 18

weather 8
wings 16
worms 8, 20